The Mighty Mechanics' Book of AMAZING FARM MACHINES

First published in 2025
by Hungry Tomato Ltd
F15, Old Bakery Studios, Malpas Road, Truro,
Cornwall, TR1 1QH, UK

Thanks to our editor, Julie Tofflemire.

Beetle Books is an imprint of Hungry Tomato.

A CIP catalog record for this book is available from the British Library

ISBN 9781835690956

Printed and bound in China

Discover more at
www.hungrytomato.com

Picture Credits
(abbreviations: t = top; b = bottom; m = middle; l = left; r = right; bg = background)

Wikipedia: By Wikideas1 - Own work, CC0 65tr. Shutterstock: 40-41m, 75tl. Aleksandr Rybalko 51tl; Alenul 2bl, 54-55m; Alexey Stiop 16ml; Alfmaler 60-61bg, 68-69bg; Amanita Silvicora 12-13bg, 26-27bg, 66-67bg; Anastasiia Kozubenko 76-77bg; Andrew Rybalko (characters throughout); Another77 66-67m; Assaa2215 29br; B Brown 44-45m, 72tl; BG Media 46bl; Brgfx 52-53bg; Catalin eremia 28m; Catocala7 30m; Cherdchai101 20mr; Daseaford 31m; David BISE 61tl; Dejan Dundjerski 48-49m; Deyana Stefanova Robova 26-27m; Droidworker 8-9bg, 46-47bg, 20-21bg, 34-35bg, 64-65bg, 72-73bg; Dvande 7tr, 70-71m, 71tr; Dzzoer 5(air compressor); Edge Creative 62-63bg; Gan chaonan 19tr; Gargantiopa 20-21m; Gavin Baker Photography 45tr; GLF Media 42bl; GordanD 24m, 36m; Gozzoli 60-61m; GraphicRF.com 58-59bg; Guitar Photographer 38-39m; HaDariha 48-49bg; Hanna Taniukevich 32-33m; Hans engbers 31tl; Hennadii H 42-43bg; Henryk Sadura 35br; Hrach Hovhannisyan 14-15m; Ian Dewar Photography 11tr; IGORdeyka 30-31bg; J.F.G.PHOTO 54bl; Julia Lazebnaya 36-37bg; KonstantinChristian 68ml; KOTOIMAGES 74-75m; Kwangmoozaa 18-19m; Lukas Puchrik 23bm; Madpixel 2-3bg, 6-7bg, 22-23bg, 32-33bg; Maksim Safaniuk 27tl, Safaniuk 77tl; Malika Keehl 18-19bg, 56-57bg; Marcelo F Junior 14ml; Mastak 28-29bg; Matveev Aleksandr 8-9m, 41tl; Miguel Perfectii 76-77m; My Creatives 24-25bg; Natallia Ploskaya 4(crowbar); Nidvoray 72-73m; Pand P Studio 58-59m; Paul R. Jones 56-57m; Photobac 6-7m, 62m; photodiode 37m; PhotoRK 36tl; ProStcokStudio 74-75bg; Rflsalles 56-57b (flowers); RGTimeline 67tr; S_oleg 42-43m; SAND55UG 39tr; Sanit Fuangnakhon 52-53m; Schankz 33tm; Scharfsinn 12-13m, 13tr; Sensvector 44-45bg; Sergey Ryzhov 25m; Sergi_Petruk 46-47m; SERSOLL 5(drill); Sheryl Watson 64-65m; Snapshoot freddy 22-23m; SOMCHAI DISSALUING 53tl; Sotisare 10-11bg, 40-41bg; Stefan11 2mr, 10-11m, 34-35m, 50-51m, 68-69m; StockStudio Aerials 57tr; Suwin66 59br; Terekhov igor 49tl; The8monkey 16-17bg; Tkray 38-39bg; UladzimirZuyeu 1m; Valentin Vlakov 16-17m; Varga Jozsef Zoltan 62tl; Vector pocket 4-5bg; Vector_Vision 50-51bg, 70-71bg; Vereshchagin 63m; Warren Design 9mr; WATCHAYUT BAMRUNGTHAI 4(grease gun); YUCALORA 54-55bg; Yura Tarasovskyy 25tr.

Every effort has been made to trace the copyright holders and we apologize in advance for any unintentional omissions.
We would be pleased to insert the appropriate acknowledgment in any subsequent edition of this publication.

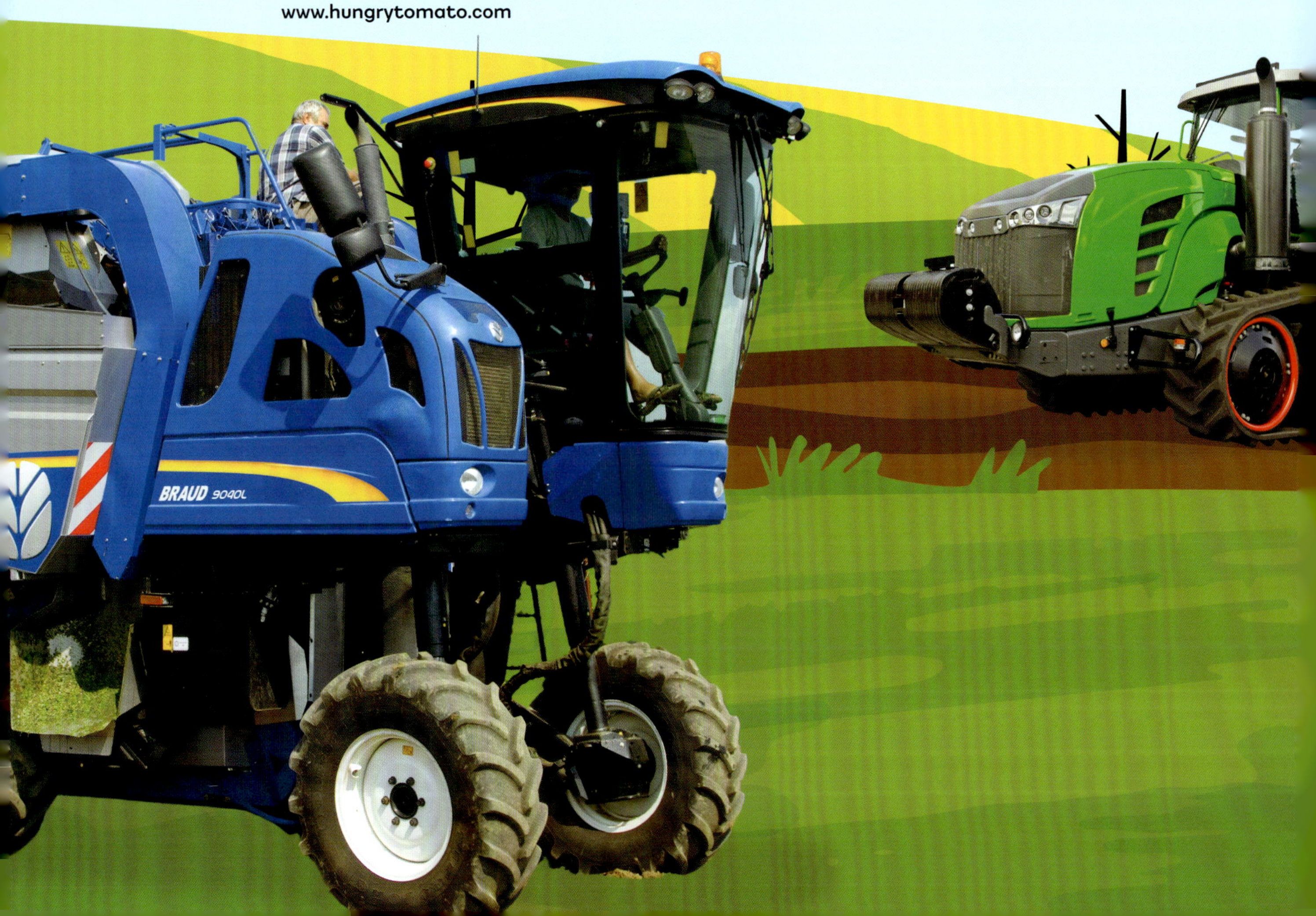

Contents

Words that appear in **bold** are explained in the glossary.

The Mighty Mechanics

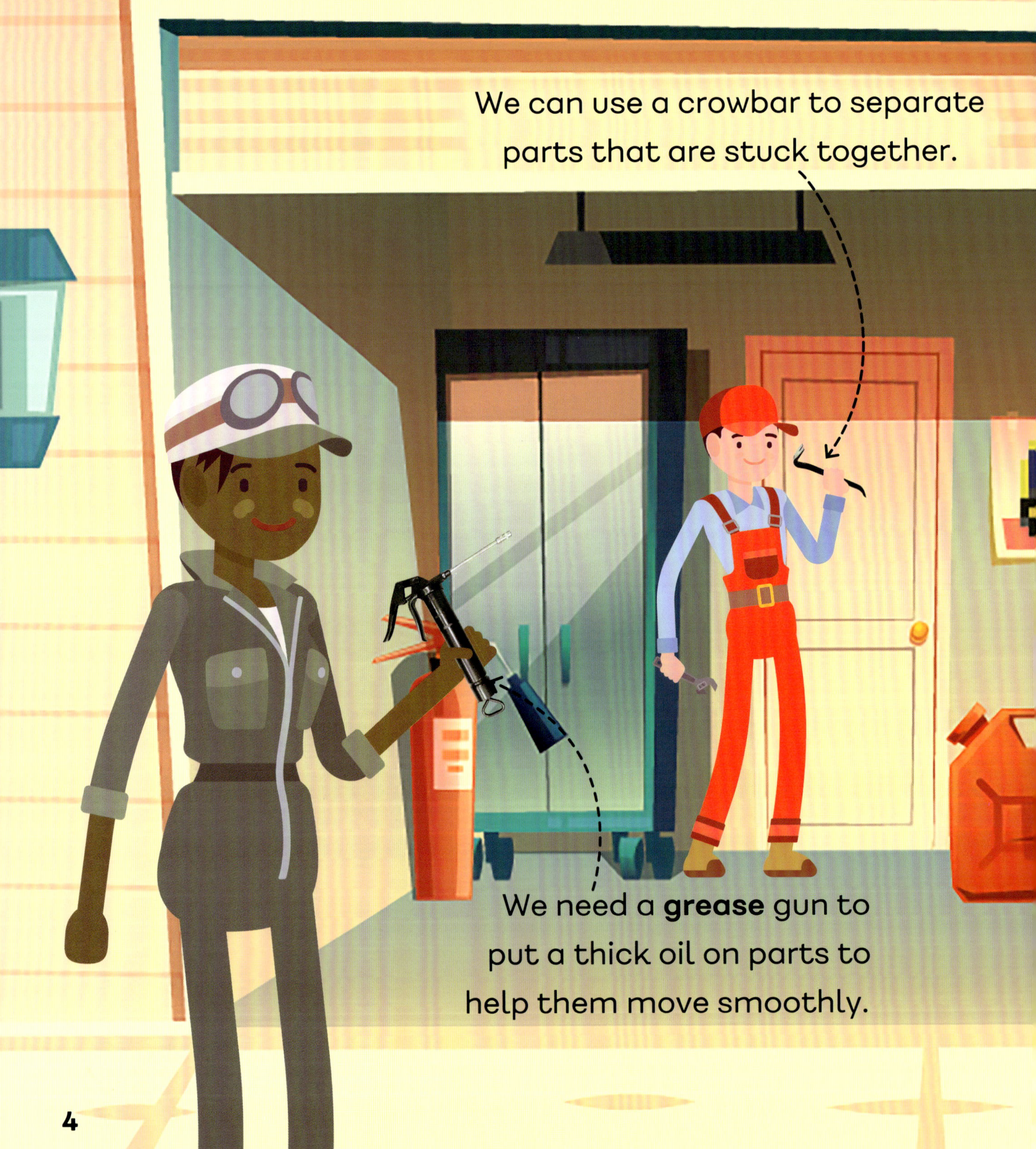

We can use a crowbar to separate parts that are stuck together.

We need a **grease** gun to put a thick oil on parts to help them move smoothly.

We are the Mighty Mechanics. Welcome to our workshop! We work on some amazing vehicles and machines. Here are a few of the tools we use to fix them.

This drill can tighten screws on equipment.

An air compressor puts air into the tires (tyres) of the farm vehicles.

Utility Tractor

A utility tractor is one of the most useful vehicles on the farm! It does a lot of different jobs.

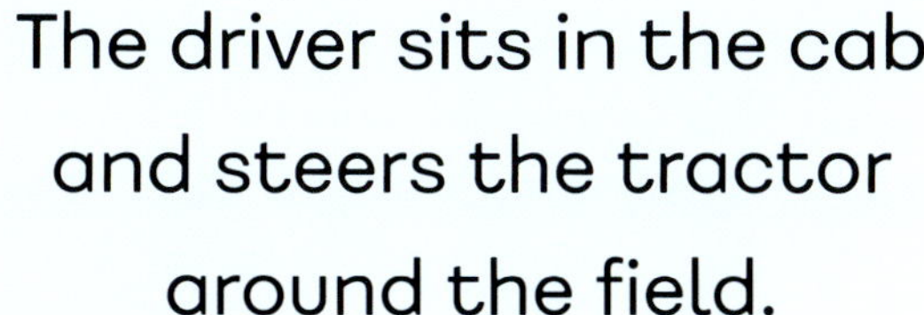

The driver sits in the cab and steers the tractor around the field.

This tractor is pulling equipment to plant seeds.

The big wheels in the back help it to move on soft ground.

Compact Tractor

For smaller jobs, a compact tractor is just the right size. It can fit into smaller spaces than a utility tractor.

The exhaust pipe removes smoke and gases from the tractor's engine.

The patterns on the tires (tyres) help them to **grip** the ground.

Crawler Tractor

This vehicle knows how to stay on track! The crawler tractor has tracks instead of wheels.

This crawler tractor is pulling equipment that breaks up the soil.

A weight at the front keeps the tractor from tipping backward.

Smart Tractor

A smart tractor is high-tech! It uses computers, a **GPS**, and sensors to do farm work. It can get a lot of work done by itself.

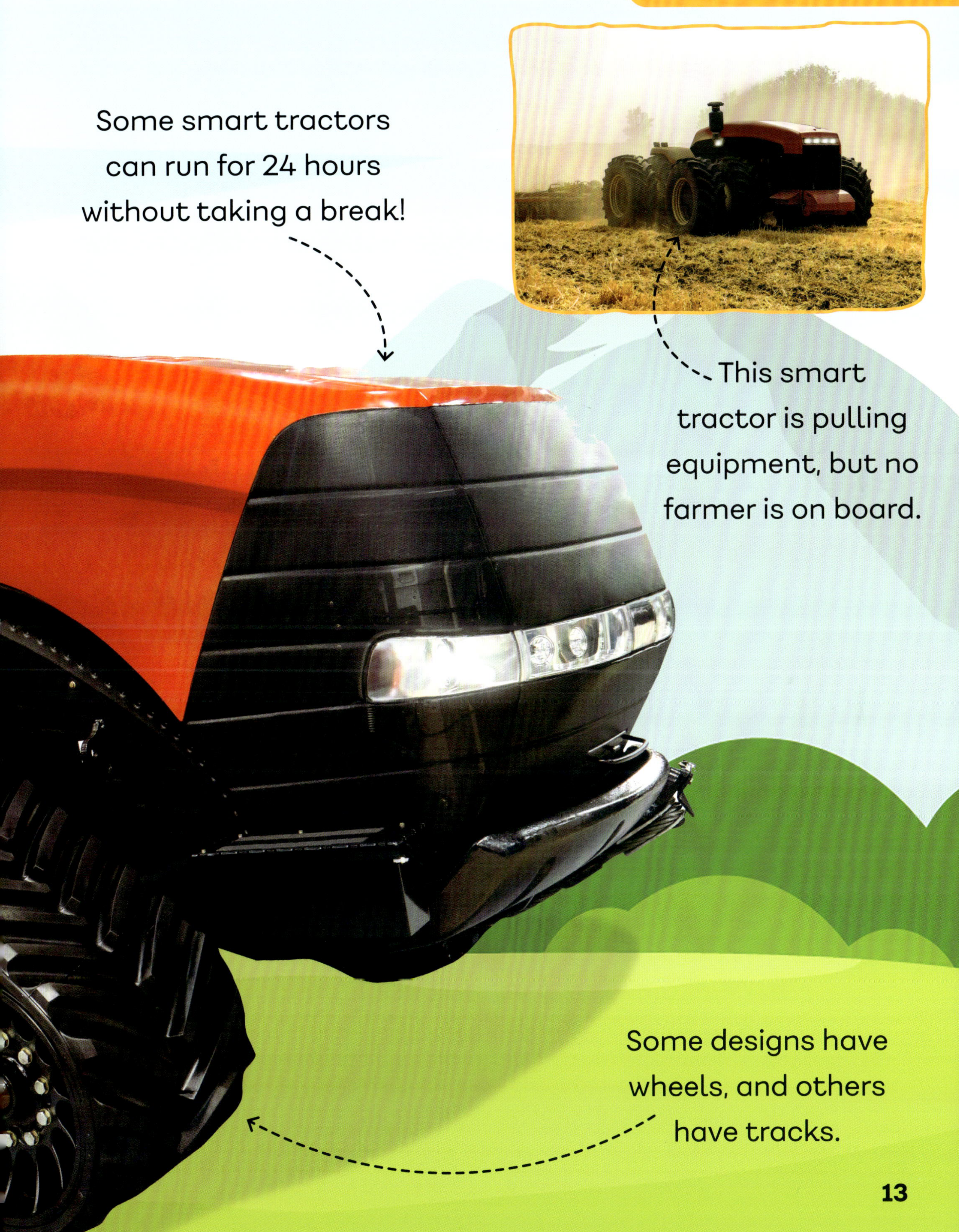

Some smart tractors can run for 24 hours without taking a break!

This smart tractor is pulling equipment, but no farmer is on board.

Some designs have wheels, and others have tracks.

Pickup Truck

A pickup truck has an open back, and it can drive on rough ground. It is strong enough to carry tools, hay, and even animals.

Some farms are enormous! Farmers need trucks to get around.

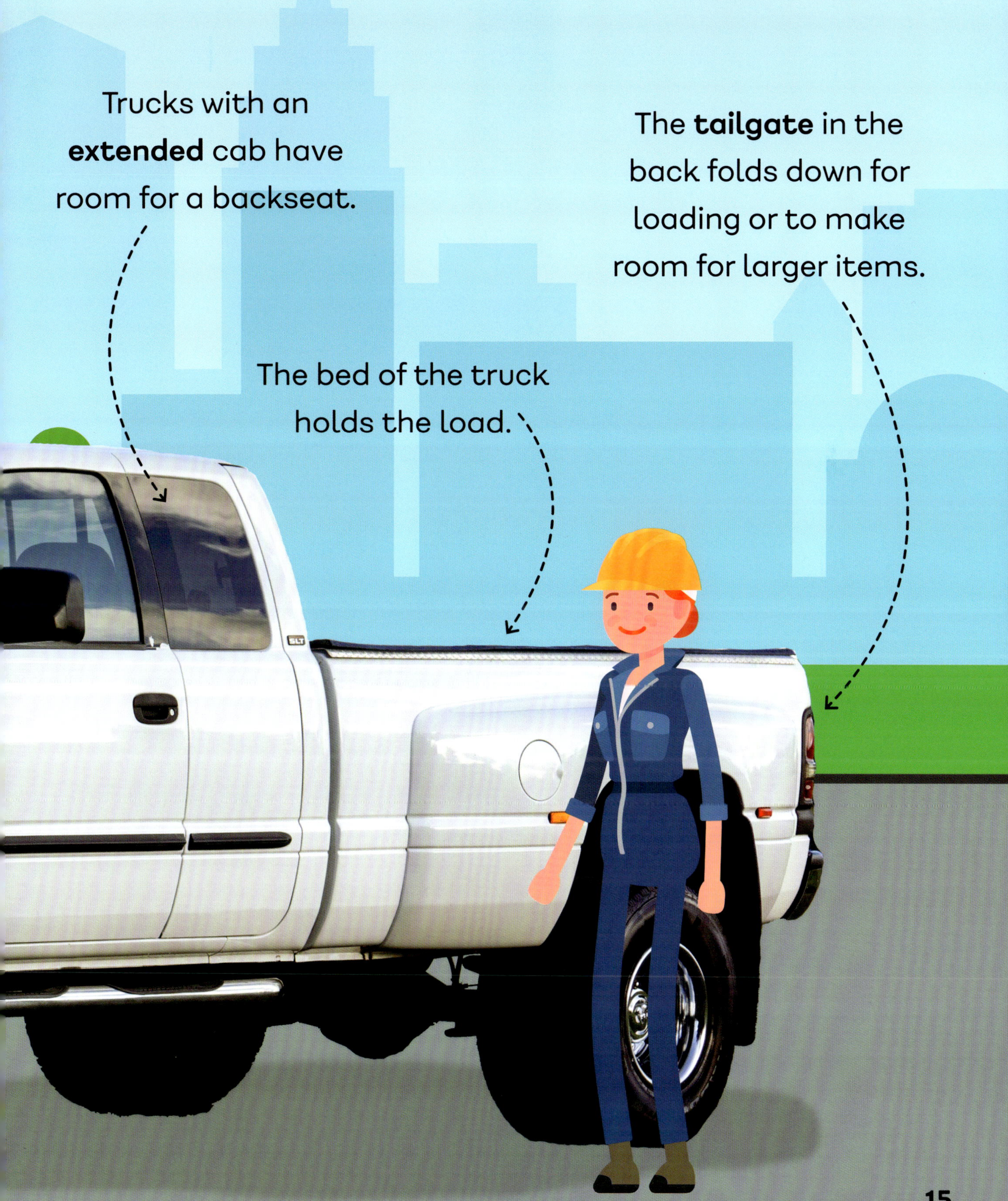

Trucks with an **extended** cab have room for a backseat.

The **tailgate** in the back folds down for loading or to make room for larger items.

The bed of the truck holds the load.

All-Terrain Vehicle (ATV)

An all-**terrain** vehicle – often called an ATV or quad bike – is tough! It can handle almost any kind of ground, so farmers can get around quickly.

This farmer is using an ATV to **herd** animals!

The driver doesn't need to push any pedals, so there are footrests for their feet.

The brakes are on the handlebars, and so is the **throttle**, which makes the vehicle go.

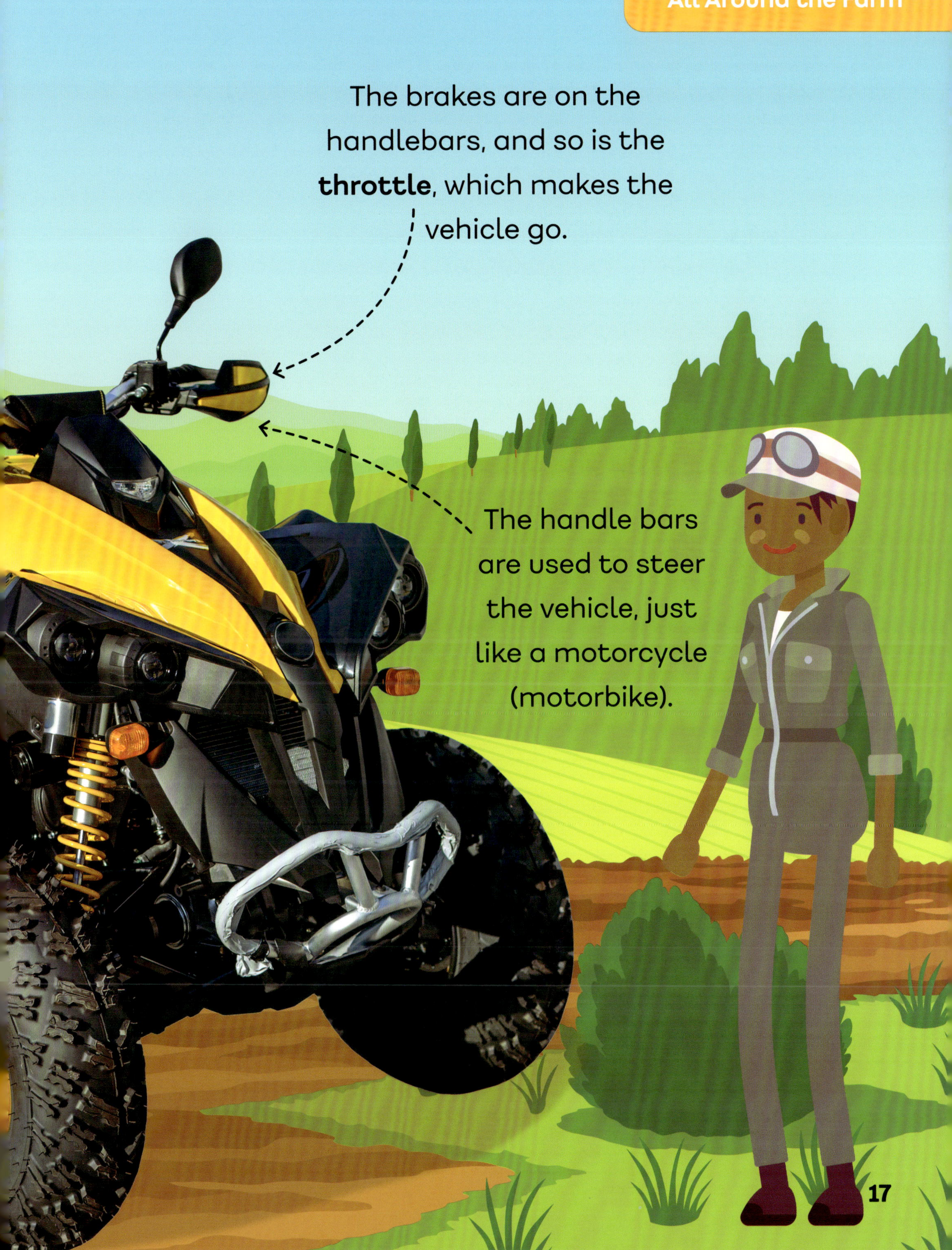

The handle bars are used to steer the vehicle, just like a motorcycle (motorbike).

Agricultural Drone

An agricultural drone is a flying robot! It can take pictures of **crops**, drop seeds, and spray fields.

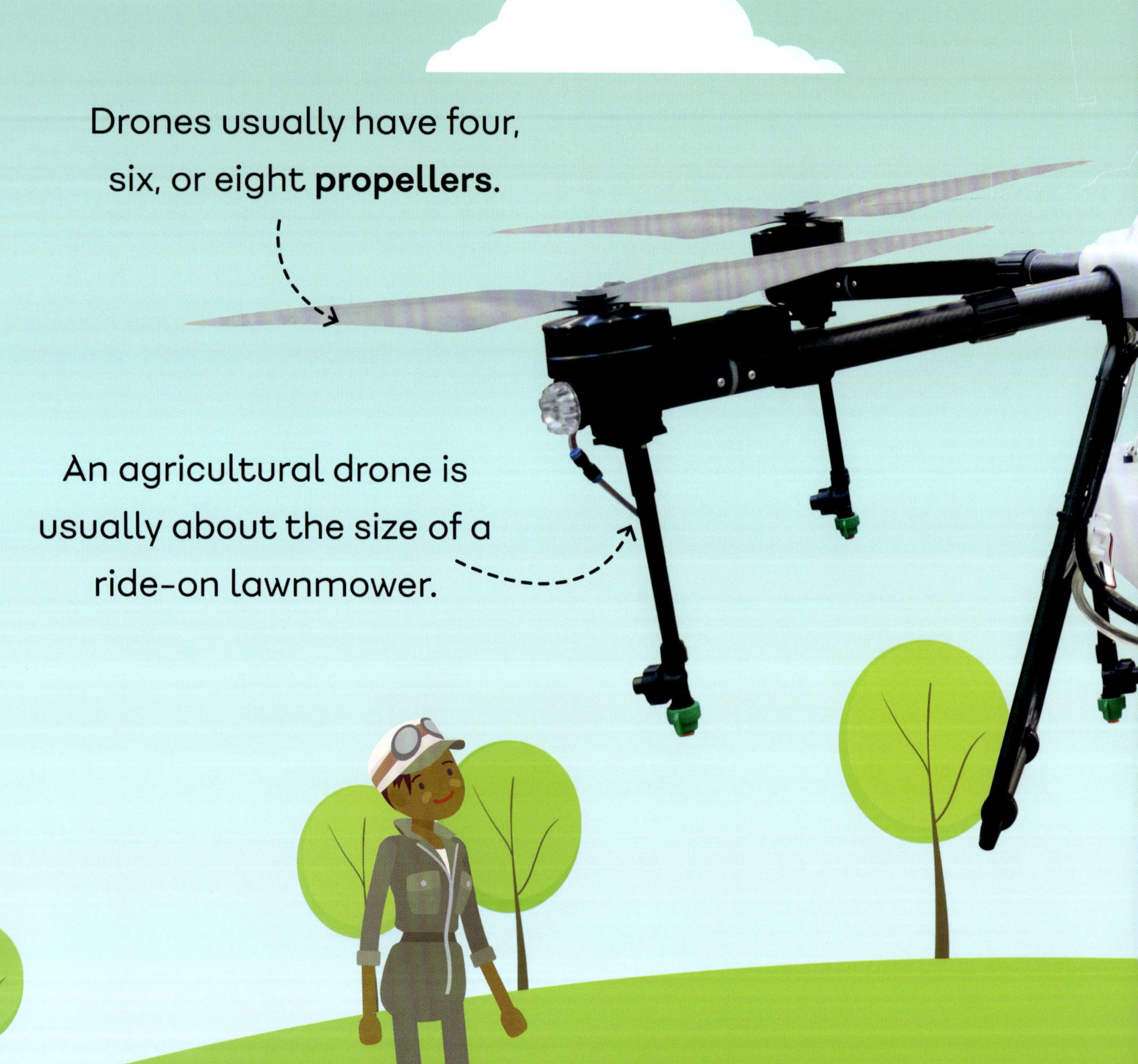

Drones usually have four, six, or eight **propellers**.

An agricultural drone is usually about the size of a ride-on lawnmower.

Drones can work in the field even if the farmer is far away.

The motor gives the drone power and makes the propellers spin.

The drone's tank holds **liquids** that can help plants grow or stop weeds.

Skid Steer Loader

A skid steer loader lifts, moves, and digs things! It is great for jobs with hay, **grain**, dirt, or food for the animals.

This skid steer loader is pushing harvested rice into a pile.

The bucket can scoop up heavy loads again and again.

Skid steer loaders can spin in a circle, so they are good for working in small spaces.

The boom arms move up and down to lift the bucket.

Weather Station

Farmers need to know a lot about the weather so they can take care of their crops. A weather station gives them the information they need.

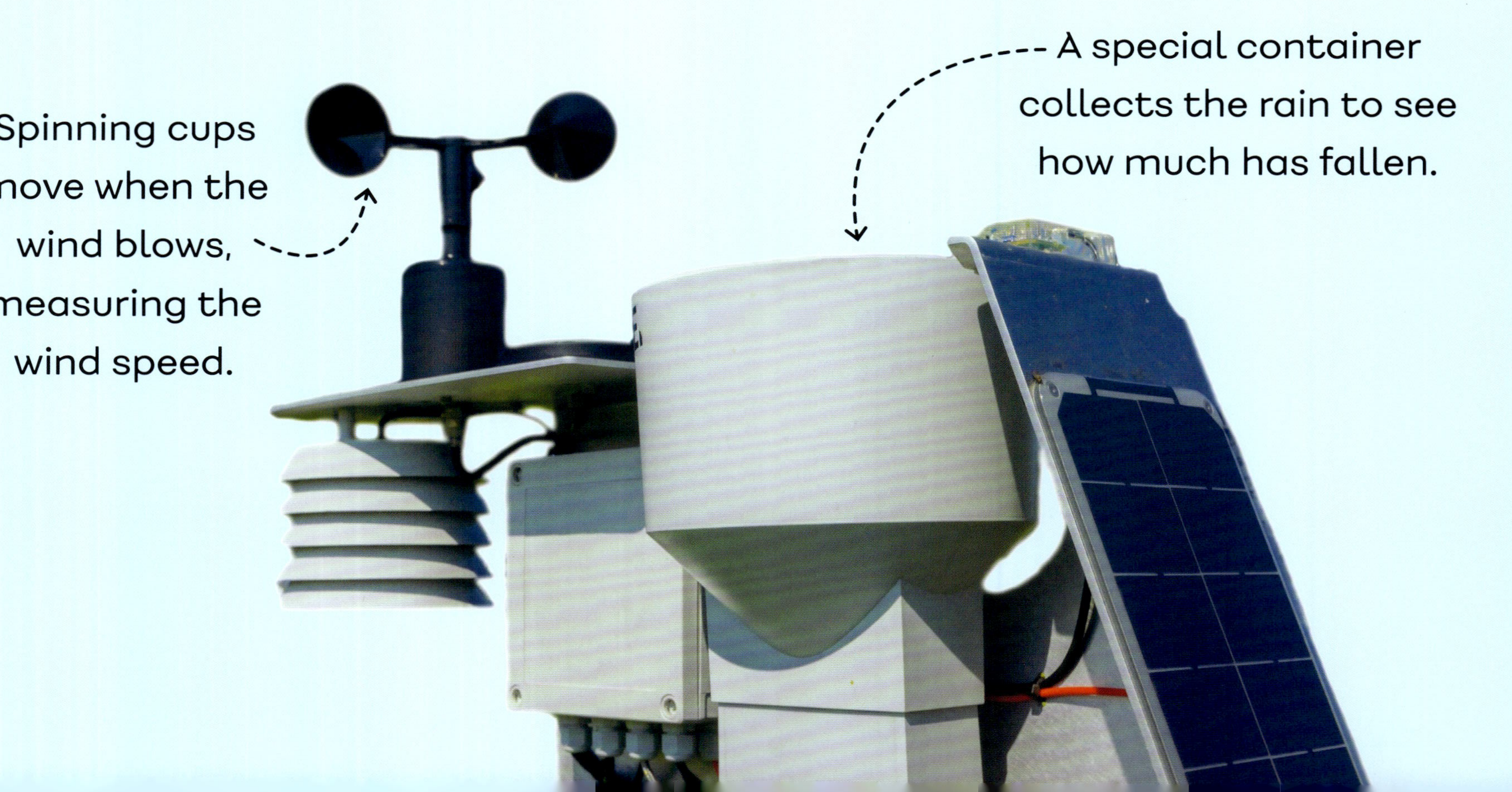

Spinning cups move when the wind blows, measuring the wind speed.

A special container collects the rain to see how much has fallen.

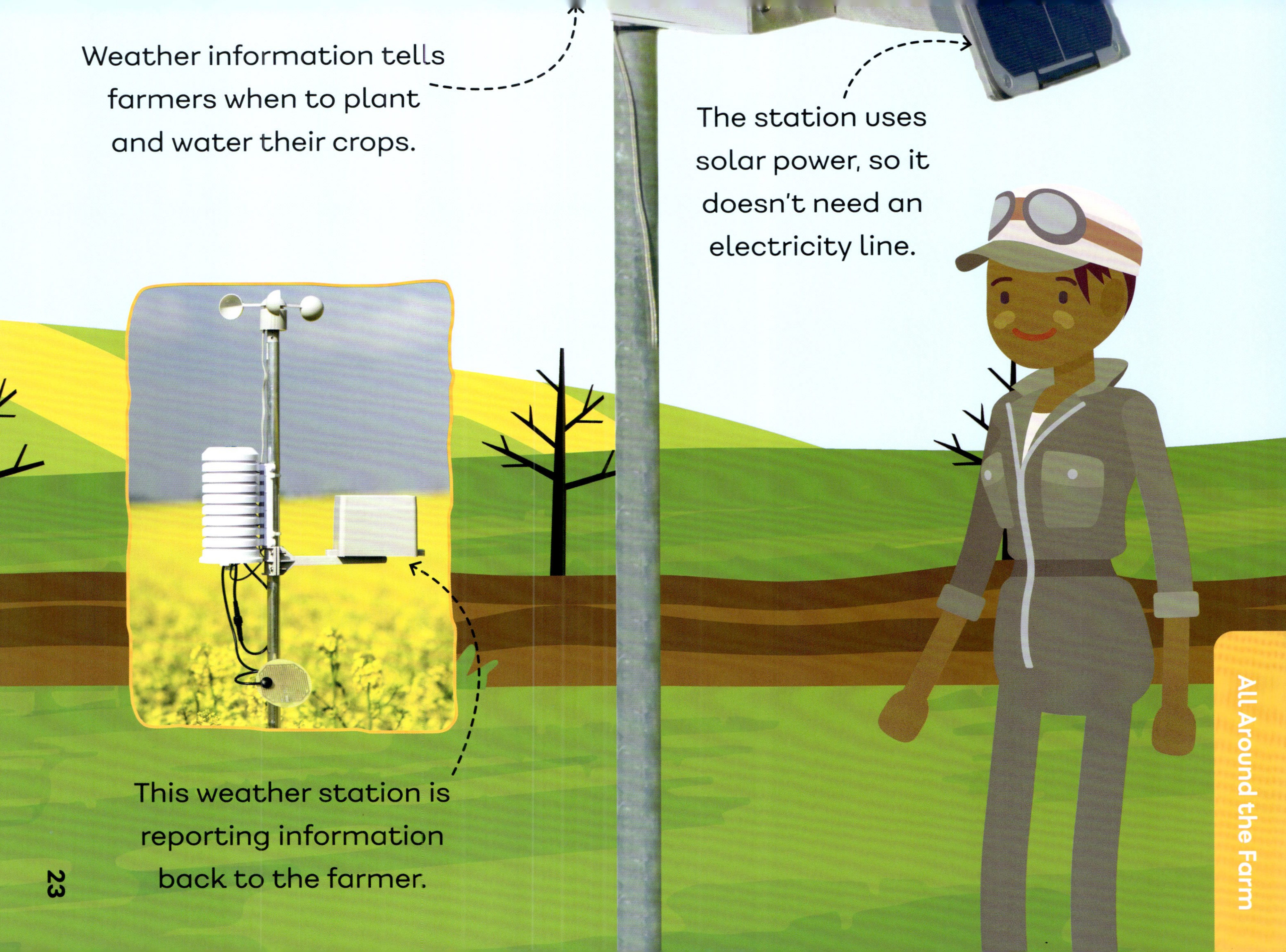
Weather information tells farmers when to plant and water their crops.
The station uses solar power, so it doesn't need an electricity line.
This weather station is reporting information back to the farmer.

Subsoiler

A subsoiler is a digging tool that is attached to the back of a tractor. It breaks up the hard soil deep in the ground.

The soil on top hardly moves, and only a cut on the **surface** is left behind.

The **shanks** on the subsoiler are like big, strong claws!

A subsoiler can be set to dig deeper or shallower.

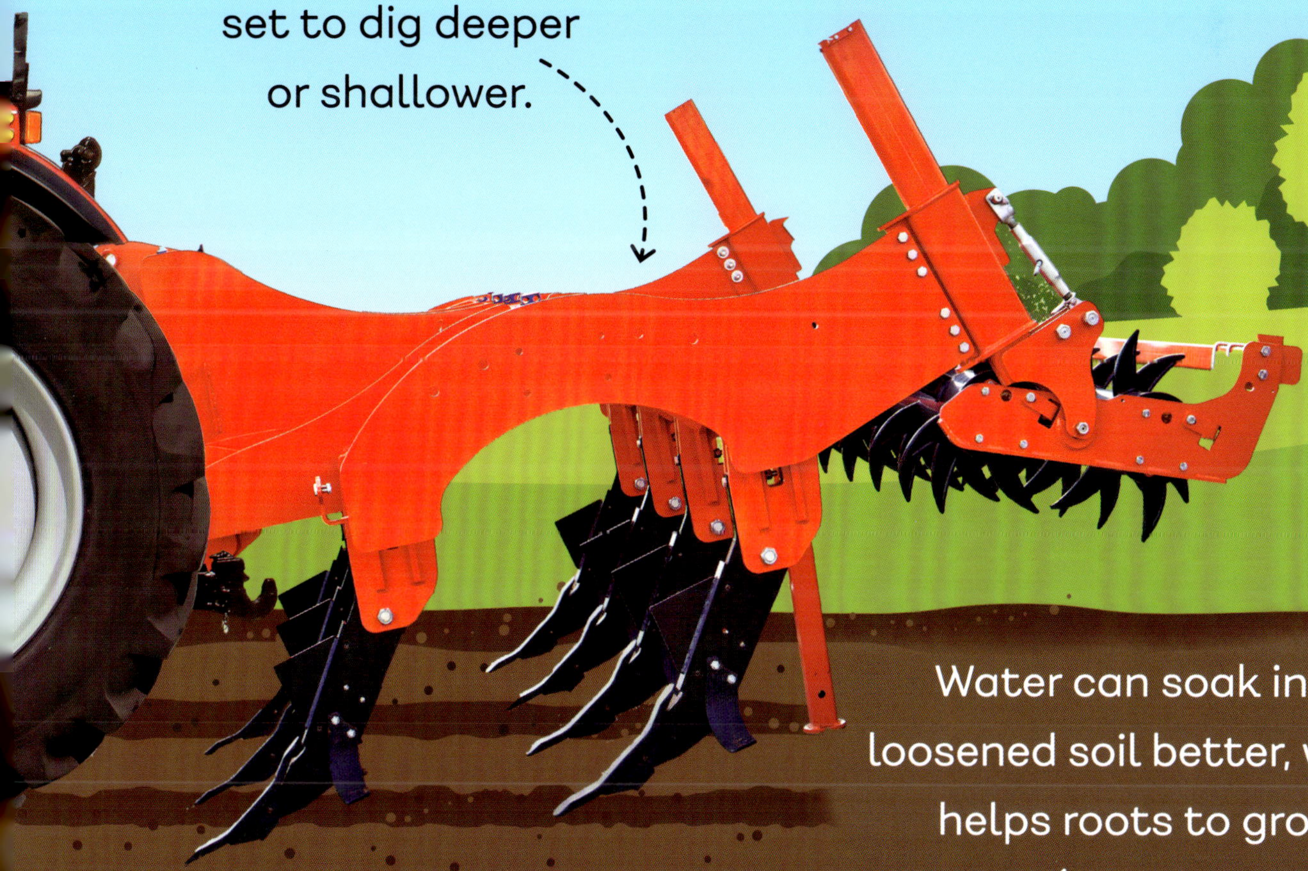

Water can soak into loosened soil better, which helps roots to grow.

Disc Harrow

A disc harrow is a huge farm tool with round, sharp **blades**. The blades cut and mix the soil to get it ready for planting.

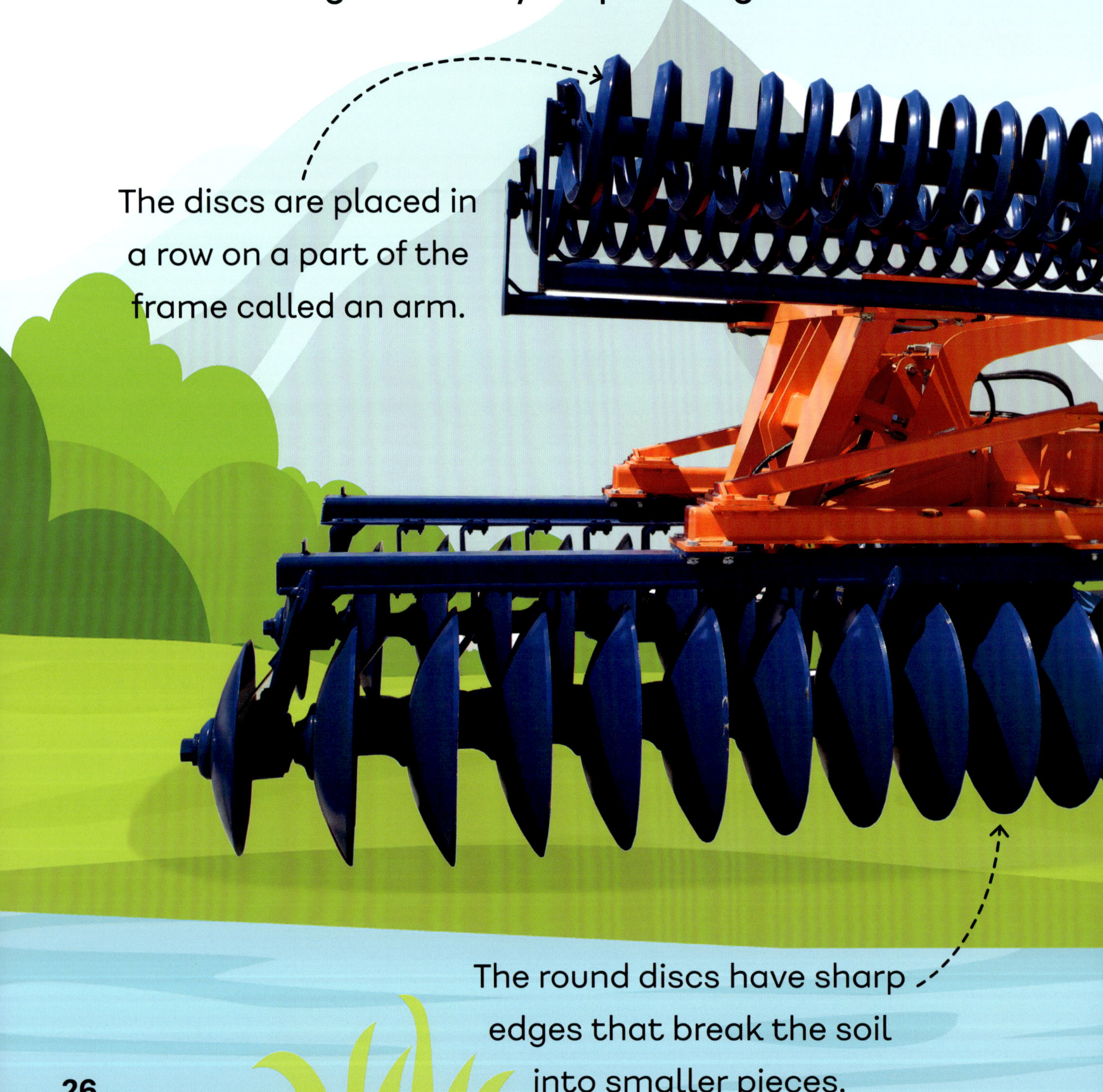

The discs are placed in a row on a part of the frame called an arm.

The round discs have sharp edges that break the soil into smaller pieces.

Weeds don't stand a chance! They get chopped up and buried.

The arms fold up for easy storage.

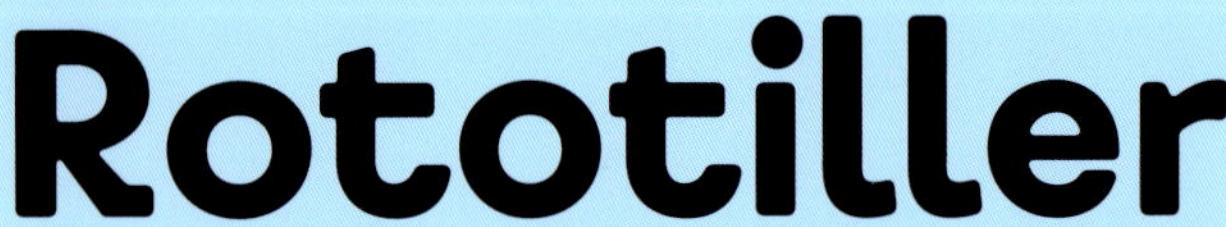

Rototiller

For smaller digging jobs, farmers can use a rototiller. It breaks up the soil and makes it loose.

The machine can mix **nutrients** into the soil too.

A small wheel (or wheels) can help move the machine across the ground.

Handles

The farmer pushes and steers using the handles.

The blades spin around quickly and dig into the soil.

Liquid Manure Spreader

Manure – that is, animal poop – is very useful on the farm. The manure spreader gets the manure to the right place.

This spreader is adding manure to the soil.

A pump moves the manure through delivery tubes.

A big tank holds the liquid manure.

The manure gives the soil nutrients and helps the plants grow.

Earth Auger

An earth **auger** is a big drill that makes deep holes in the ground. Farmers use it to build fences or plant young trees.

This auger is digging a hole for a fence post!

Handles help the farmer to hold it steady.
A small tank is filled with gas (fuel) to give the machine power.
The **spiral**-shaped bit pulls up dirt as it spins.

Chain Trencher

A chain trencher cuts long, narrow holes in the soil. Farmers use it to bury **irrigation** pipes and create **trenches** for water to flow.

This chain trencher is cutting through the soil like a giant chainsaw!

Seeding Machine

A seeding machine plants seeds in the soil. It spreads the seeds evenly so that each plant has enough space.

The farmer has to cover every part of the field.

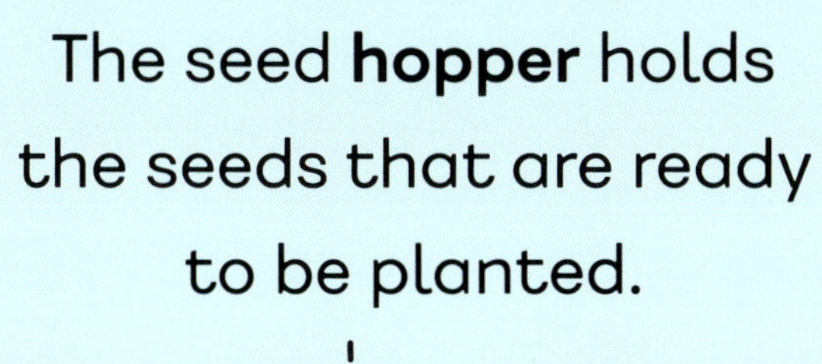

The seed **hopper** holds the seeds that are ready to be planted.

The machine makes small holes in the soil for the seeds.

Seeds travel through tubes from the hopper to the ground.

Wheels at the back push the soil back over the planted seeds.

Rice Transplanter

A rice transplanter places tiny rice plants in a wet field. The machine makes sure they have the same amount of space around them.

Seeds are planted in trays and grown for about 25-50 days to become **seedlings.**

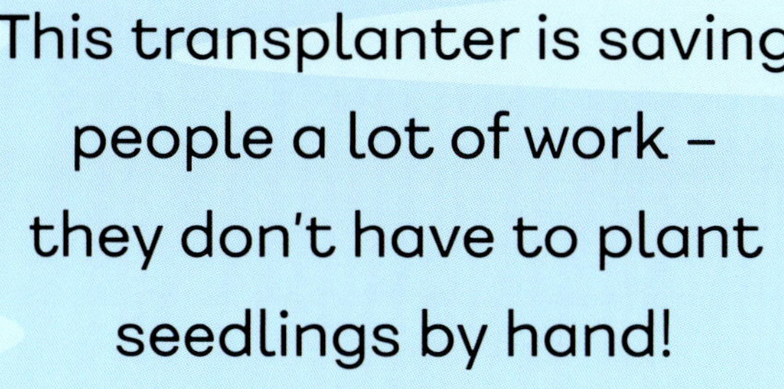

This transplanter is saving people a lot of work – they don't have to plant seedlings by hand!

The seedlings are placed in groups on the seedling rack.

The planting arms push the seedlings into the ground.

Seeding and Weeding Robot

A seeding and weeding robot plants seeds in perfect rows and pulls out weeds. It helps farmers get their work done faster!

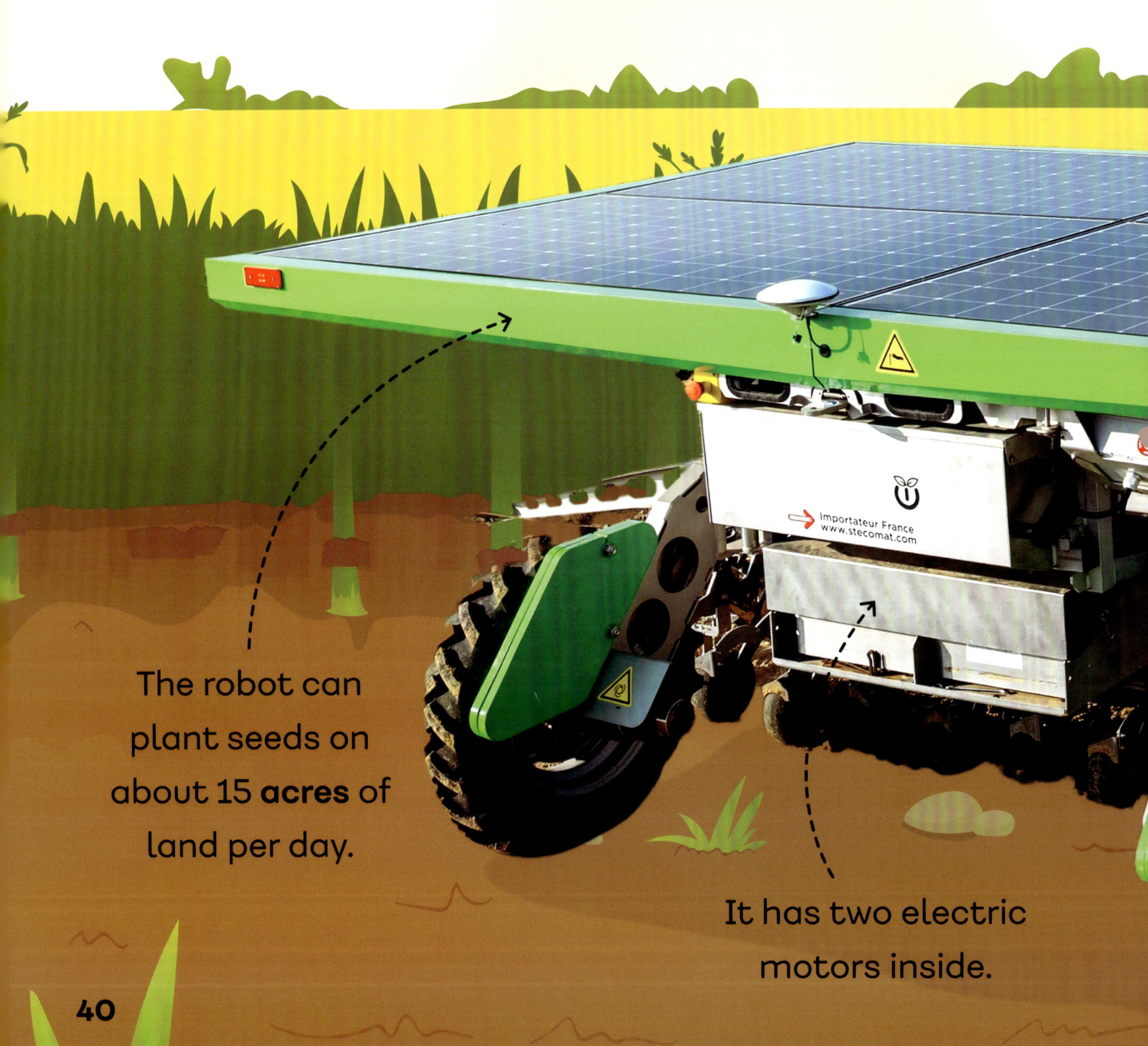

The robot can plant seeds on about 15 **acres** of land per day.

It has two electric motors inside.

There are four solar panels on top to give the vehicle power.

GPS helps the robot know exactly where to go.

Irrigation System

Crops need water, but rain doesn't always fall. An irrigation system gives crops the water they need, even when the weather is dry.

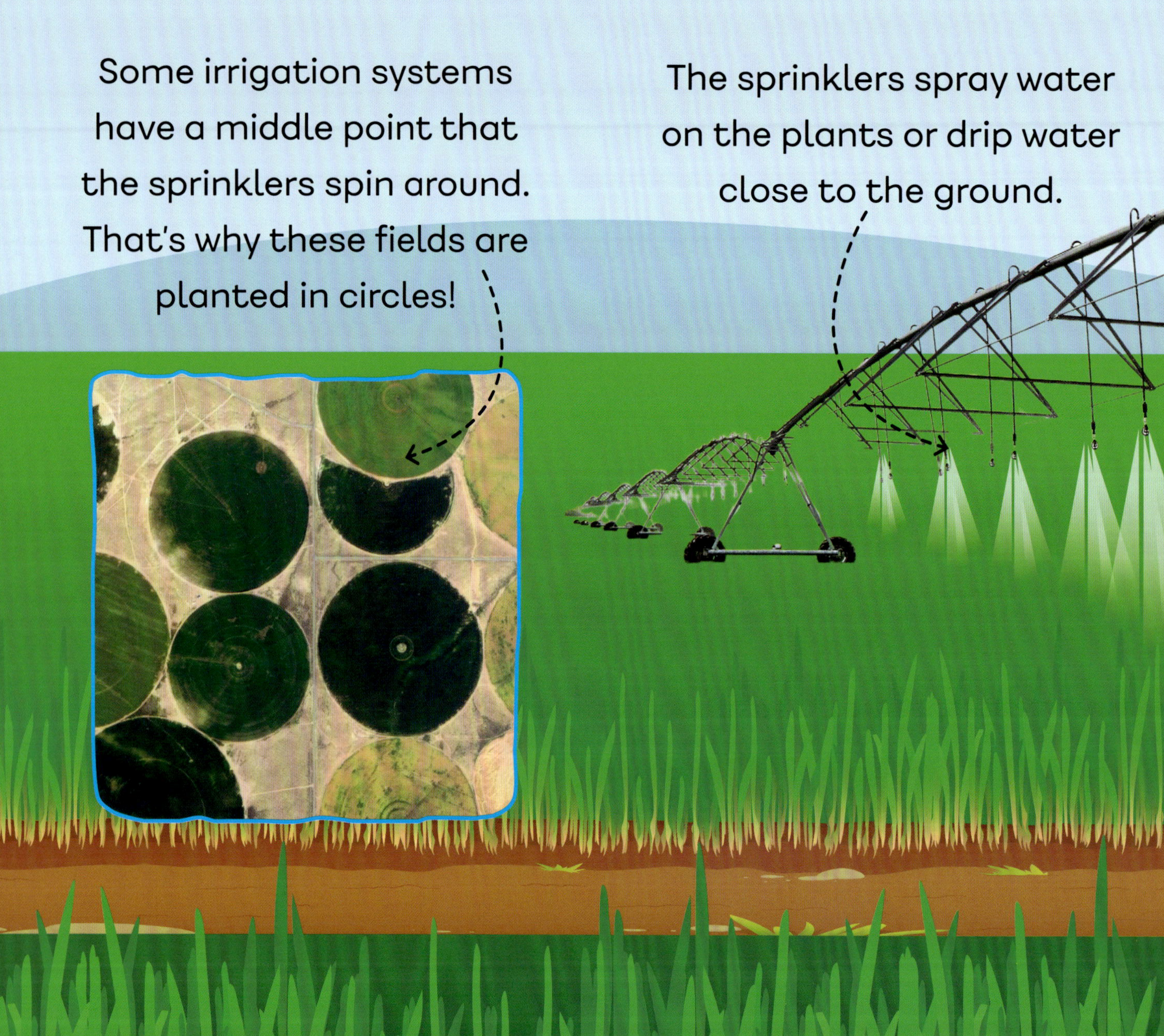

Some irrigation systems have a middle point that the sprinklers spin around. That's why these fields are planted in circles!

The sprinklers spray water on the plants or drip water close to the ground.

Water is usually pumped from the ground, a river, or a lake.

Water flows through pipes to the sprinklers.

Crop Duster

A crop duster is a small plane that flies low over fields. It sprays plant food or bug spray.

A tank inside holds the liquid.

The liquid sprays out from tiny holes under the wings.

This crop duster can cover up to 200 acres in just one hour!

The pilot flies the plane from the cockpit.

Sprayer

A sprayer spreads water, liquid plant food, or bug spray over plants. Some sprayers are pulled by tractors, but others are powered by their own engine.

Long arms, called booms, stretch out to cover a larger area.

The spray comes out of **nozzles** and is spread evenly over the field.

The tank on some sprayers can hold enough liquid to fill 50 bathtubs!

The farmer operates the sprayer from the cab.

Chicken Feeder

A chicken feeder holds food for chickens and keeps it clean. The machine keeps letting out food so the chickens always have something to eat!

A motor turns a part inside the feeder's pipe that is like a big screw.

The food drops into the feeding pan. Now the chickens can enjoy their meal!

The farmer fills the hopper with chicken food.

As it turns, the food is carried through the pipe.

Combine Harvester

A combine harvester – or combine – cuts, collects, and sorts crops all at once. It helps farmers harvest big fields quickly!

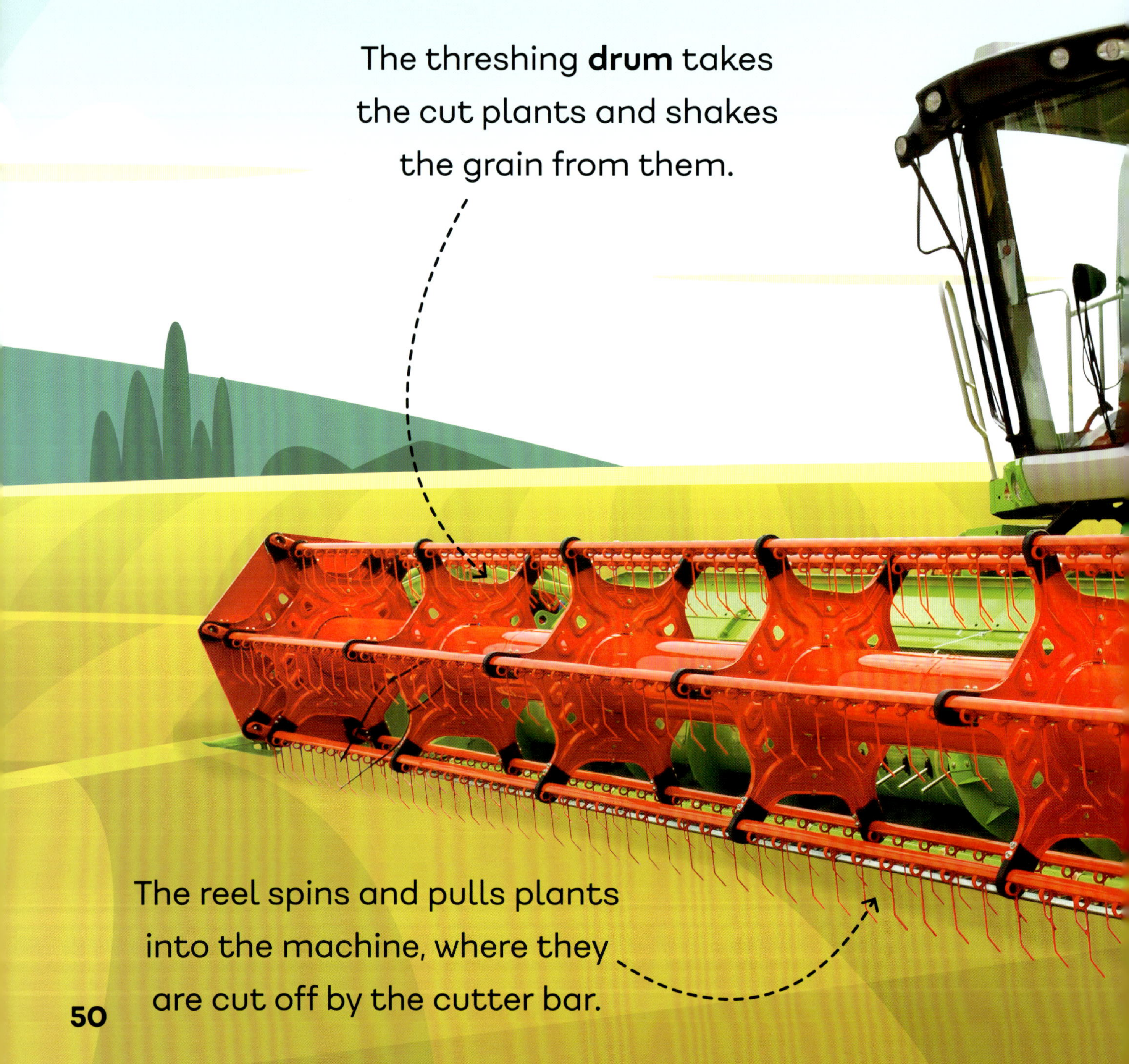

The combine's front part, called the header, can be 40 feet (12 m) wide!

The leaves and stems are separated out, and the grain falls into a collection tank.

Sugarcane Harvester

A sugarcane harvester chops down tall sugarcane plants and takes off the leaves. It collects the **stalks** so they can be made into sugar.

The sugarcane pieces are carried up a **conveyor belt** and collected in a truck.

The machine blows out the leaves, soil, and tops that are not needed.

The stalks are chopped into smaller pieces.

Grape Harvester

A grape harvester shakes vines to gently collect grapes without damaging them. Later, they might be made into juice or eaten as a snack!

The grapes land in a bin inside the vehicle.

This grape harvester can do the job of 100 workers!

The picking arms gently shake the vines to make the grapes fall off.

The grape harvester is tall so that it can roll above the vines and not hurt them.

Cotton Harvester

A cotton harvester picks the fluffy part of the cotton plant and removes the seeds. Some harvesters squeeze the cotton into modules, tightly packed shapes that are easy to store and transport.

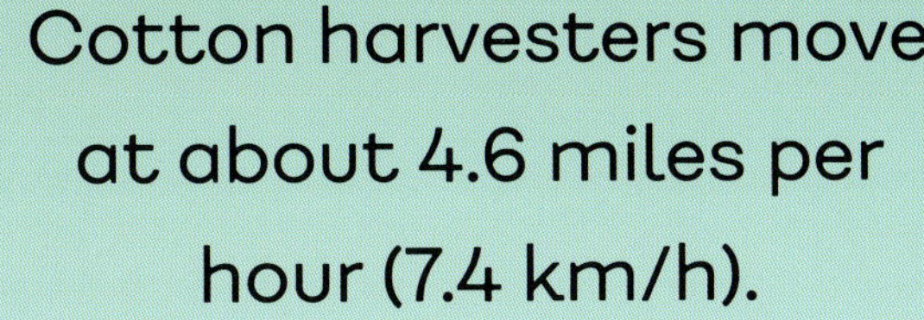

Cotton harvesters move at about 4.6 miles per hour (7.4 km/h).

Barbed rods called spindles pull the cotton off the plant.

Robot Harvester

Robot harvesters might be important farming tools in the future, though they're not used a lot yet. They can work all day and night without getting tired!

The robotic arm can move in many different directions to reach crops.

The robots have cameras and sensors that help them "see" the crops.

Artificial intelligence (AI) tells the robot when a crop is ready to be picked.

The machine pulls off the crop or cuts its stem.

Rotary Rake

A rotary rake spins to gather hay into neat rows. It helps keep hay clean and dry.

The rows, called windrows, can be picked up by a baler (see page 62) later.

A big spinning wheel with arms moves close to the ground.

Baler

A baler gathers dried grass or hay and squeezes it into tight bundles called bales. Farmers use the bales to feed animals.

The baler rolls over rows of dry hay and scoops everything up.

The finished hay bale is pushed out of the machine!

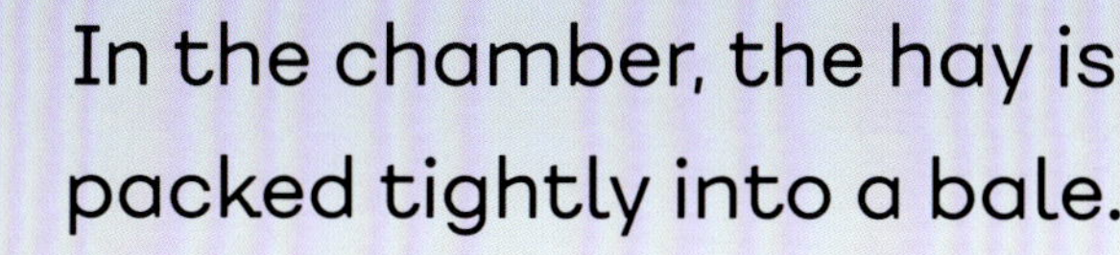

In the chamber, the hay is packed tightly into a bale.

The feeder moves the hay inside the baler.

Bale Wrapper

A bale wrapper covers hay bales in plastic. This keeps the hay dry and fresh so that animals on the farm can have food even in winter.

The bale is loaded onto the wrapper.

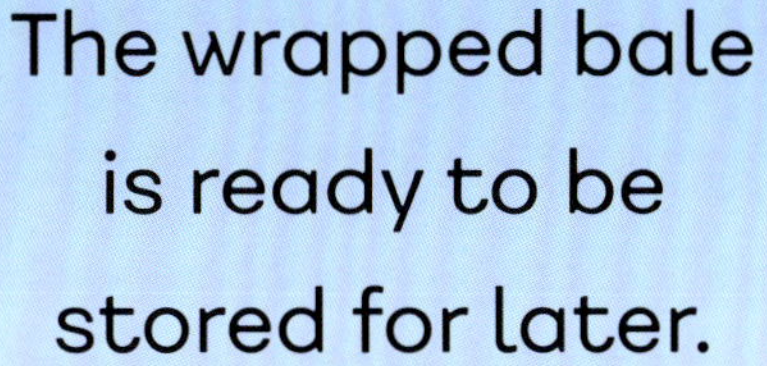

The wrapped bale is ready to be stored for later.

In-line bale wrappers make long rows of wrapped bales.

A sharp blade cuts the plastic.

Rollers spin the bale while plastic from a big roll is wrapped around it.

Forklift

A forklift lifts and moves heavy farm supplies like hay bales, seed bags, and tools. It makes carrying things much easier!

The arms lift the items up or down on the mast.

Two flat, metal forks at the front slide under items.

This forklift is moving a stack of hundreds of onions!

A heavy block at the back keeps the vehicle from tipping forward.

Telescopic Handler

A telescopic handler – or telehandler – is like a forklift but with a long arm. It lifts things high up or far away.

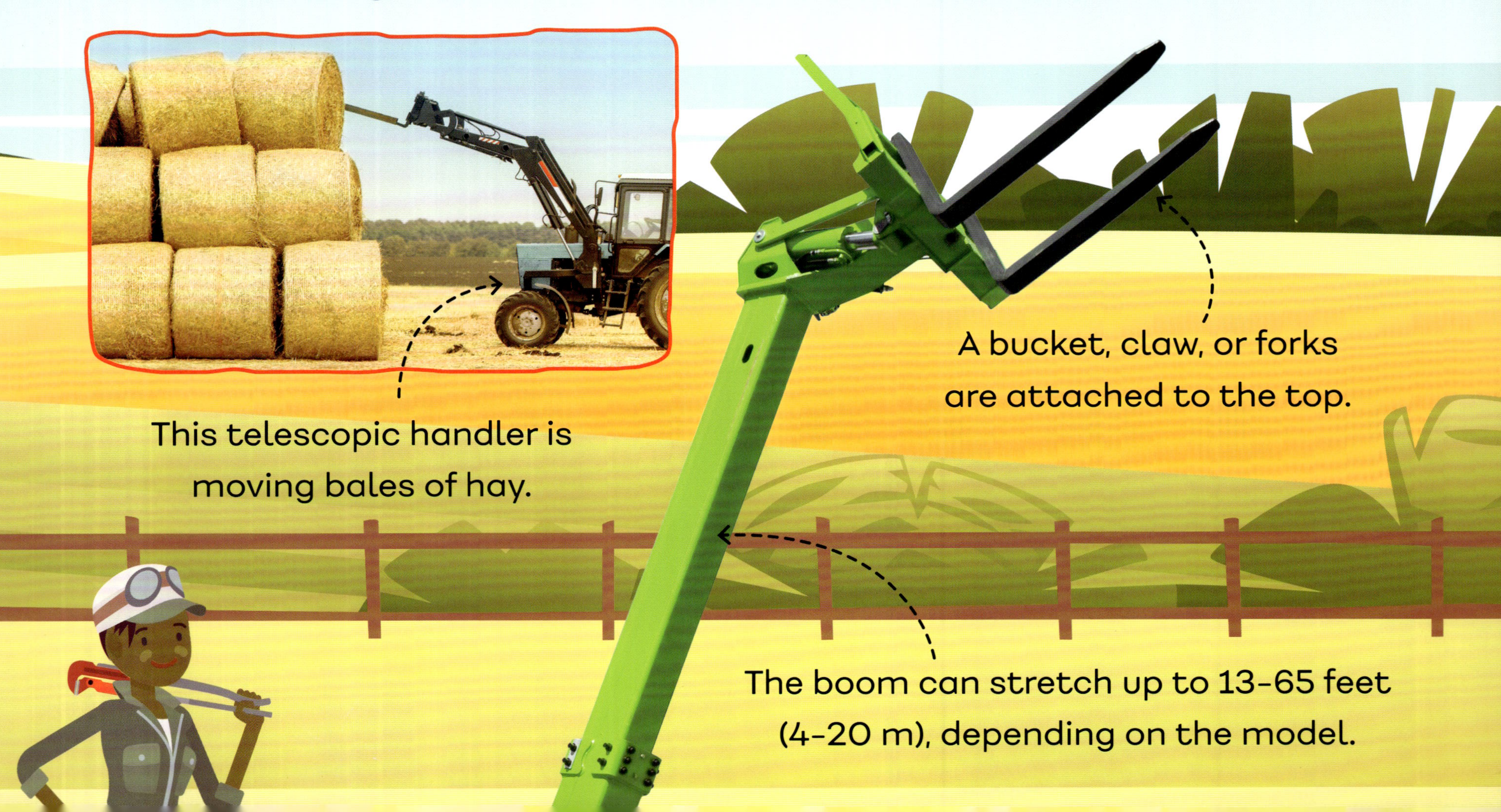

This telescopic handler is moving bales of hay.

A bucket, claw, or forks are attached to the top.

The boom can stretch up to 13–65 feet (4–20 m), depending on the model.

Special legs called outriggers can extend out to the ground to make the vehicle more stable.

Grain Cart

A grain cart carries harvested grain from the field to a storage area. It can hold a lot of grain.

Once the grain is collected, an auger moves the grain out of the cart.

A tractor pulls the cart alongside a harvester to catch the harvested crops.

This grain cart is helping a combine harvester with the corn harvest.

Grain is caught and stored in the hopper, ready to be moved off the field.

Grain Auger

A grain auger is a long pipe that moves grain into **silos**, trucks, or bins. It gets the grain from the ground to a higher place.

This grain auger is filling a silo with grain.

Grain is dumped into the hopper low to the ground.

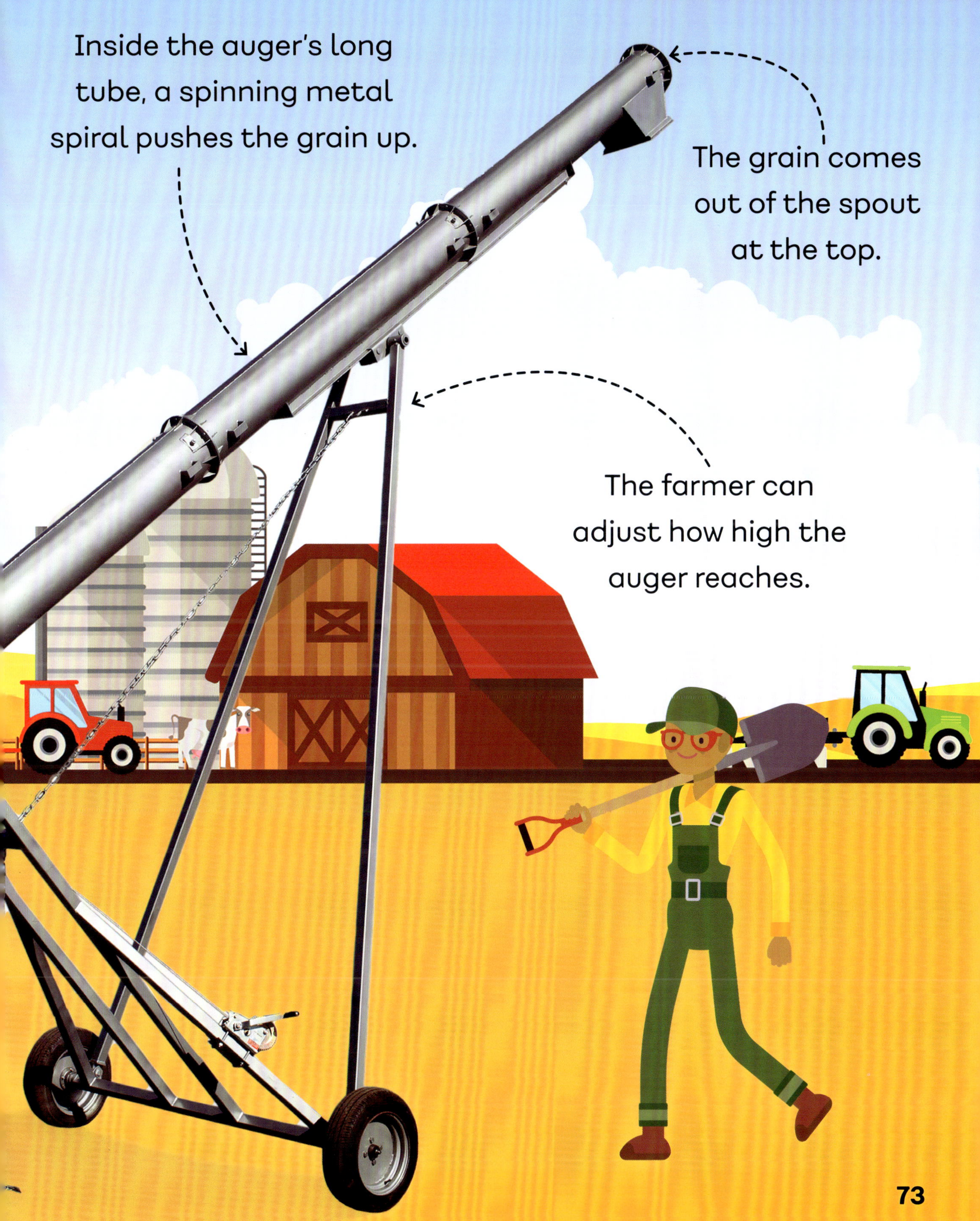
Inside the auger's long tube, a spinning metal spiral pushes the grain up.
The grain comes out of the spout at the top.
The farmer can adjust how high the auger reaches.

Milk Tanker

A milk tanker is a huge truck that carries fresh milk from farms to factories. It keeps the milk cold and safe along the way.

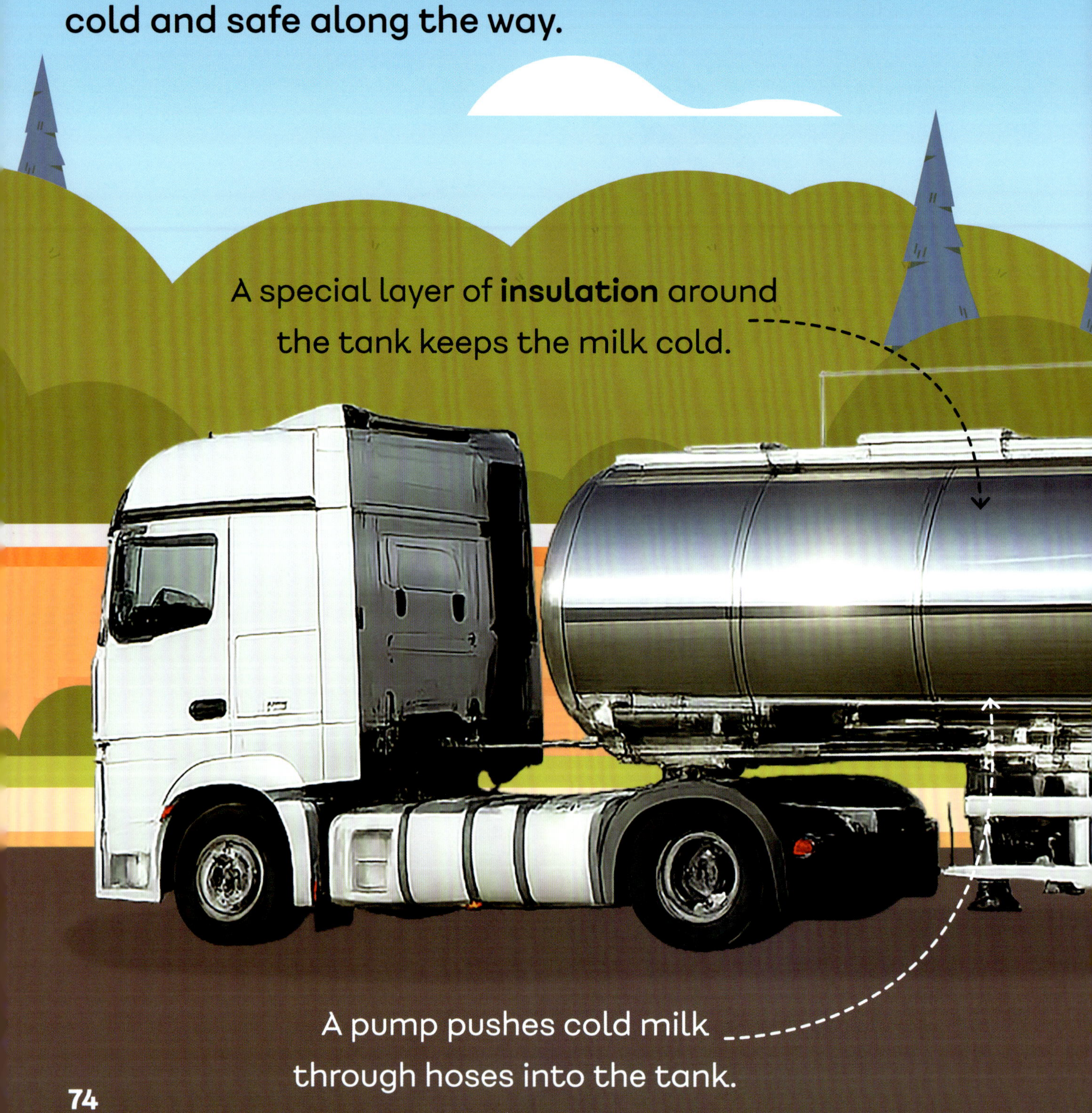

The milk is pumped back out again when it is delivered.

Drivers have to be careful because milk can **slosh** around while turning or braking!

The tank can hold 5,000 gallons (22,730 L) of milk or more!

Livestock Transporter

A livestock transporter is a special truck that moves cows, pigs, and other farm animals.

The animals ride in a big metal box called a trailer.

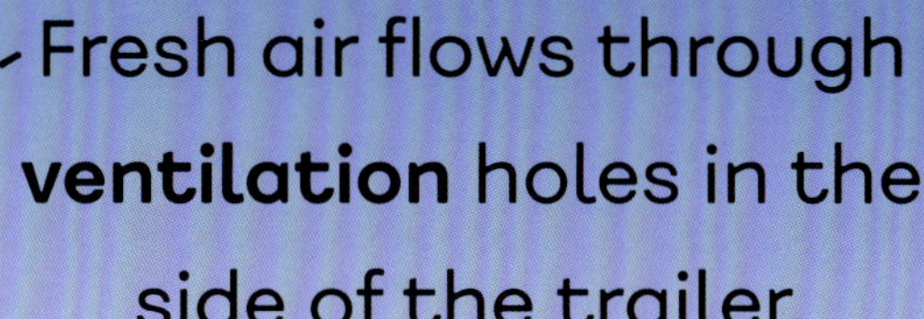

Fresh air flows through **ventilation** holes in the side of the trailer.

Ramps at the back help the animals to walk into or out of the trailer.

Walls inside the trailer keep the animals in smaller groups.

Glossary

Acre – a unit for measuring land that is 43,560 square feet (4047 sq m). You can fit about 16 tennis courts in an acre.

Artificial intelligence (AI) – computer systems that can think and learn like humans.

Auger – a tool shaped like a screw that can dig holes or move things through a tube.

Barbed – having sharp points or hooks.

Blades – flat, sharp tools for cutting.

Conveyor belt – a moving strip that carries things from one place to another.

Crops – plants grown for food.

Drum – a large container with round ends and long, straight sides.

Extended – something that has been made longer.

Grain – small, hard seeds from food plants such as rice or wheat.

Grip – to hold tightly.

GPS – Global Positioning System, a system that uses satellites in space to find the exact location of something.

Grease – a thick, oily material often used to make machines run more smoothly.

Herd – to make animals come together in a group.

Hopper – a container in a V shape that lets things out through the bottom.

Insulation – a material that is wrapped around something to keep heat, electricity, sound, etc. out.

Irrigation – using pipes to supply water to land.

Liquids – substances that flow freely such as water, juice, or milk.

Nutrients – substances such as vitamins that help living things grow and be healthy.

Nozzles – small pieces at the end of a pipe that spray out liquids (see "liquids").

Propellers – long, flat parts on a plane that turn to make the plane move forward.

Shanks – straight, narrow parts of a tool that can dig.

Seedlings – young plants.

Sensors – a machine part that notices changes around it in things like light, temperature, or movement, and sends this information to other devices.

Silo – a tall tower that is used for storing grain.

Slosh – when liquids move carelessly or noisily (see "liquids").

Stalks – the main stems of plants.

Surface – the top part or layer of something.

Spiral – a shape that is a curved line that goes around a central point. The line around a screw is a spiral.

Tailgate – a door at the back of a vehicle that opens downward.

Terrain – ground or land.

Throttle – the part that controls how much fuel goes into an engine and makes the vehicle go.

Trenches – long, deep holes.

Ventilation – the fact of letting fresh air come in and move around.

Index